Lumbar Spinal STABILIZATION

Floor Exercises

2nd Edition

Donald R. Murphy, DC
with Gary F. Ierna, DC

The authors have made every effort to ensure the accuracy of the information herein, in particular with regard to the protocols and procedures of the specific exercise tracks. No patient however should perform any of these exercises without proper instruction from their doctor or therapist. The authors disclaim any responsibility for any adverse effects resulting directly or indirectly from the suggested protocols, undetected errors, or the readers misunderstanding of this text.

All inquiries should be addressed to:
OPTP
P.O. Box 47009
Minneapolis, MN 55447
800.367.7393
OPTP.com

ISBN #978-0-9904230-2-7

Table of Contents

01. Preparation

02. Supine Track

Table of Contents (continued)

03. Bridge Track

04. Quadruped Track

05. Lunge/Squat Track

01 Preparation

EXERCISE 1.1 Finding the Neutral Spine Position

Lie on your back with your knees and hips bent and your feet resting comfortably on the floor. This is known as the "hook lying" position (figure 1).

Figure 1

Slowly rock your pelvis backward as if you were pressing the small of your back against the floor (unless your health care provider has instructed you to avoid this movement) (figure 2).

Now slowly rock your pelvis forward as if you were pressing your rear end against the floor while lifting your abdomen (unless your health care provider has instructed you to avoid this movement) (figure 3). Be sure to keep the movements slow and controlled. Explore the entire range of movement in both directions. If you are currently in pain, identify those points in the range of movement in which the pain is increased, decreased or eliminated.

Figure 2

To identify the neutral spine position, repeat the previous movement by rocking your pelvis as if you were pressing your rear end against the floor while lifting your abdomen (figure 3). Then back away from this position to a point at which your spine is resting comfortably. This is the neutral spine position. All of the following exercises should be done in the neutral spine position.

Figure 3

EXERCISE **1.2** Co-contraction Maneuver

Lie on your back in the hook lying position and establish the neutral spine position (figure 1).

Figure 1

Co-contraction maneuver means to gently pull your belly button straight back toward your spine (figure 2). Be sure not to raise your chest while you are doing this. This may be difficult at first, but remain as relaxed as possible and you will find that this makes it easier.

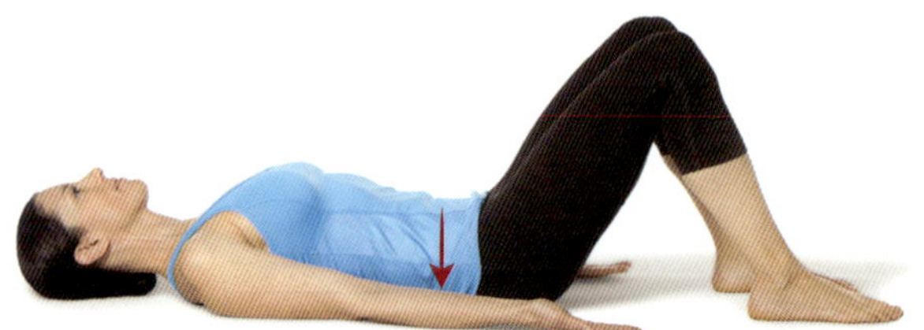

Figure 2

It is important <u>not</u> to "suck in your gut" (figure 3) but rather to gently pull your belly button backward. If you have difficulty doing this from the hook lying position, try doing it on your hands and knees.

Figure 3 Incorrect movement.

EXERCISE **1.3** Co-contraction Maneuver: Quadruped Position

From the hands and knees position establish the neutral spine position. Be sure to keep a normal curve in your lower back (figure 1). To perform the co-contraction maneuver, gently pull your belly button straight back toward your spine (figure 1). Keep your head aligned with the rest of your body. Avoid letting your chin poke out toward the floor. This may be difficult at first, but remain as relaxed as possible and you will find that this makes it easier.

Figure 1

If you are still not sure if you are correctly performing the co-contraction maneuver in the quadruped position, a "trick" that can be applied is to co-contract indirectly by activating the pelvic floor muscles.

EXERCISE **1.4** Activating the Pelvic Floor Muscles

Lie on your back in the hook lying position and establish the neutral spine position (figure 1).

Figure 1

Imagine you are urinating and gently try to stop the flow of urine. This activates the muscles of the pelvic floor and, indirectly, the deep muscles of the spine and abdomen.

Another "trick" that further enhances this is to press your tongue against the roof of your mouth, just behind the front teeth, and maintain that pressure while you are performing the maneuver.

EXERCISE **1.5** Brugger

Sit on a chair with your "sit bones" at the edge. Have your feet turned outward and your legs apart. Rock your pelvis forward into a tilt so that your belly juts slightly forward. Slightly tuck your chin, open your fingers wide and turn your hands outward so that your thumbs are pointing behind you. Be sure to keep your fingers as wide as possible (figure 1).

Figure 1

Hold this position for 5-10 seconds, and then relax. Repeat this exercise ________ times. This position should be taken periodically throughout the day, especially if you are spending a great deal of time sitting.

02 Supine Track

EXERCISE **2.1** Supine Single Arm Raise

From the hook lying position, maintain the neutral spine position and the co-contraction maneuver. Have your arms elevated so that your fingers are pointing straight up toward the ceiling (figure 1).

Slowly lower your right arm until it is all the way overhead (figure 2). Be sure to maintain the neutral spine position and the co-contraction maneuver while you do this.

Slowly return to the starting position, and repeat this movement with the left arm.

Repeat ________ times on each side.

Figure 1

Figure 2

EXERCISE **2.2** Supine Double Arm Raise

From the hook lying position, maintain the neutral spine position and the co-contraction maneuver. Have your arms elevated so that your fingers are pointing straight up toward the ceiling (figure 1).

From here slowly lower both arms overhead without losing the neutral spine position or co-contraction maneuver (figure 2).

Slowly return to the starting position.

Repeat ________ times.

Figure 1

Figure 2

EXERCISE **2.3** Supine Single Leg Raise

From the hook lying position, maintain the neutral spine position and the co-contraction maneuver (figure 1).

Slowly raise your right leg until your hip is bent to 90 degrees (figure 2). Be sure to maintain the neutral spine position and the co-contraction maneuver while you do this.

Slowly return to the starting position, and repeat this movement with the left leg.

Repeat ________ times on each side.

Figure 1

Figure 2

EXERCISE **2.4** Supine Single Leg Extension

From the hook lying position, maintain the neutral spine position and the co-contraction maneuver (figure 1).

Slowly lift your right leg and then extend it straight out (figure 2). Be sure to maintain the neutral spine position and the co-contraction maneuver while you do this.

Bring it back to the starting position. Then repeat this movement with the left leg.

Repeat ________ times on each side.

Figure 1

Figure 2

EXERCISE **2.5** Supine Single Arm and Leg Raise

From the hook lying position, maintain the neutral spine position and the co-contraction maneuver. Have your arms elevated so that your fingers are pointing straight up toward the ceiling (figure 1).

Figure 1

Slowly lower your left arm to the floor and raise your right leg to the 90 degrees position at the same time (figure 2). The other arm and leg should remain stationary. Be sure to maintain the neutral spine position and the co-contraction maneuver while you do this.

Slowly bring the arm and leg back to the starting position, and repeat with the right arm and left leg.

Repeat ________ times on each side.

Figure 2

EXERCISE **2.6** Supine Alternating Kicks

Lie on your back with your hips and knees bent and your feet in the air (figure 1). Maintain the neutral spine position and the co-contraction maneuver.

Figure 1

Slowly extend your left leg straight out while keeping your right leg bent at 90 degrees (figure 2). Be sure to maintain the neutral spine position and the co-contraction maneuver while you do this.

Return your leg to the starting position and repeat with your right leg.

Repeat ________ times on each side.

Figure 2

EXERCISE **2.7** Dead Bug

Lie on your back with your hips and knees bent, your feet in the air and your arms extended straight out in front of you (figure 1). Maintain the neutral spine position and the co-contraction maneuver.

Figure 1

Slowly lower your left arm over your head while you slowly extend your right leg straight out; keep your left leg bent at 90 degrees (figure 2). The other arm and leg should remain stationary. Be sure to maintain the neutral spine position and the co-contraction maneuver while you do this.

Return to the starting position and repeat with your right arm and left leg.

Repeat ________ times on each side.

Figure 2

EXERCISE **2.8** Supine Pelvic Rotation With Feet On the Floor

Lie on your back with your hips and knees bent and your feet on the floor. Extend arms out to the sides at 90 degrees. Maintain the neutral spine position and the co-contraction maneuver (figure 1).

Figure 1

Slowly rotate your legs and pelvis to the right so that your knees move halfway to the floor (figure 2). Be sure to maintain the neutral spine position and the co-contraction maneuver while you do this.

Straighten up again and repeat to the other side.

Repeat ________ times on each side.

Figure 2

EXERCISE **2.9** Supine Pelvic Rotation With Feet Off the Floor

Lie on your back with your hips and knees bent and your feet in the air. Extend arms out to the sides at 90 degrees. Maintain the neutral spine position and the co-contraction maneuver (figure 1).

Figure 1

Slowly rotate your legs and pelvis to the right so that your knees move halfway to the floor (figure 2). Do not touch the floor, but come as close as you can without pain. Be sure to maintain the neutral spine position and the co-contraction maneuver while you do this.

Straighten up again and repeat to the other side.

Repeat ________ times on each side.

Figure 2

EXERCISE **2.10** Curl Ups

Lie on your back with your hips and knees bent and your feet on the floor. Maintain the neutral spine position and the co-contraction maneuver. Have your arms crossed in front of your chest (figure 1).

Figure 1

Slowly raise your chest up so that your upper back curves (figure 2). Keep your chin slightly tucked throughout the movement. Be sure to maintain the neutral spine position and the co-contraction maneuver while you do this.

Slowly lower yourself back down to the floor.

Repeat ________ times.

Figure 2

03 Bridge Track

EXERCISE **3.1** Basic Bridge

From the hook lying position, maintain the neutral spine position and the co-contraction maneuver (figure 1).

Slowly raise your pelvis off the floor into the bridge position (figure 2). Be sure to maintain the neutral spine position and the co-contraction maneuver while you do this.

Slowly lower back to the starting position.

Repeat ________ times.

Figure 1

Figure 2

EXERCISE **3.2** Bridge with Strap

From the hook lying position, wrap a strap or belt around your legs just above the knees. Maintain the neutral spine position and the co-contraction maneuver (figure 1).

Slowly raise your pelvis off the floor into the bridge position (figure 2). Be sure to maintain the neutral spine position and the co-contraction maneuver while you do this.

Slowly lower back to the starting position.

Repeat ________ times.

Figure 1

Figure 2

EXERCISE **3.3** Bridge With Heel Raises

From the bridge position, maintain the neutral spine position and the co-contraction maneuver (figure 1).

Slowly raise your right heel off the floor (figure 2). Be sure to maintain the neutral spine position and the co-contraction maneuver.

Slowly lower back to the starting position. Repeat with the left heel.

Repeat ________ times on each side.

Figure 1

Figure 2

EXERCISE **3.4** Bridge With Steps

From the bridge position, maintain the neutral spine position and the co-contraction maneuver (figure 1).

Slowly raise your right foot approximately 1" off the floor (figure 2). Be sure to maintain the neutral spine position and the co-contraction maneuver.

Slowly lower back to the starting position. Repeat with the left foot.

Repeat ________ times on each side.

Figure 1

Figure 2

EXERCISE **3.5** Bridge With Leg Extension

From the bridge position, maintain the neutral spine position and the co-contraction maneuver (figure 1).

Slowly extend your right leg until it is straight (figure 2). Be sure to maintain the neutral spine position and the co-contraction maneuver while you do this.

Slowly lower back to the starting position. Repeat with the left leg.

Repeat ________ times on each side.

Figure 1

Figure 2

EXERCISE **3.6** One Leg Bridge

From the bridge position, maintain the neutral spine position and the co-contraction maneuver (figure 1).

Extend your right leg until it is straight (figure 2).

Slowly lower your pelvis back down to the floor (figure 3). Be sure to maintain the neutral spine position and the co-contraction maneuver while you do this.

Raise your pelvis back up to the starting position. Repeat with the left leg.

Repeat ________ times on each side.

Figure 1

Figure 2

Figure 3

EXERCISE **3.7** Side Bridge with Bent Knees

Lie on your side, propped up on your forearm (figure 1). Maintain the neutral spine position and the co-contraction maneuver. Have your knees bent so that your feet are behind you. Your body from head to knee should be in a straight line.

Push your pelvis up a few inches from the floor (figure 2).

Slowly lower yourself back down to the floor.

Repeat ________ times. Then switch sides and repeat motion.

If you have trouble with this exercise at first, try it with one hand on the floor for support (figure 3).

Figure 1

Figure 2

Figure 3

EXERCISE **3.8** Side Bridge with Straight Knees

Lie on your side, propped up on your forearm with your legs straight (figure 1). Maintain the neutral spine position and the co-contraction maneuver. Your body from your head to your feet should be in a straight line.

Push your pelvis up a few inches from the floor (figure 2).

Slowly lower yourself back down to the floor.

Repeat ________ times. Then switch sides and repeat motion.

If you have trouble with this exercise at first, try it with one hand on the floor for support (figure 3).

Figure 1

Figure 2

Figure 3

04 Quadruped Track

EXERCISE **4.1** Quadruped Single Arm Raise

From the hands and knees position, maintain the neutral spine position and the co-contraction maneuver. Be sure to keep a normal curve in your lower back and keep your head aligned with the rest of your body (figure 1). Avoid letting your chin poke out toward the floor.

Figure 1

From this position, raise your left arm out in front of you (figure 2). Be sure to maintain the neutral spine position and the co-contraction maneuver while you do this.

Return your arm to the floor and repeat with the right arm.

Figure 2

Repeat ________ times on each side.

EXERCISE **4.2** Quadruped Single Leg Raise

From the hands and knees position, maintain the neutral spine position and the co-contraction maneuver. Be sure to keep a normal curve in your lower back and keep your head aligned with the rest of your body (figure 1). Avoid letting your chin poke out toward the floor.

Figure 1

From this position, extend your left leg behind you (figure 2). Be sure to maintain the neutral spine position and the co-contraction maneuver while you do this.

Return your leg to the floor and repeat with the right leg.

Repeat ________ times on each side.

Figure 2

EXERCISE **4.3** Quadruped Cross-Crawl

From the hands and knees position, maintain the neutral spine position and the co-contraction maneuver. Be sure to keep a normal curve in your lower back and keep your head aligned with the rest of your body (figure 1). Avoid letting your chin poke out toward the floor.

Figure 1

From this position, raise your right arm out in front of you while, at the same time, you extend your left leg behind you (figure 2). Be sure to maintain the neutral spine position and the co-contraction maneuver while you do this.

Figure 2

Return your arm and leg to the floor and repeat with the left arm and right leg.

Repeat ________ times on each side.

EXERCISE **4.4** Plank

From the hands and knees position, maintain the neutral spine position and the co-contraction maneuver.

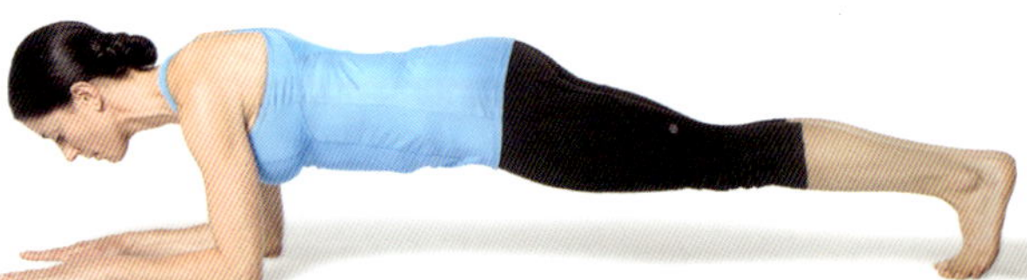

Figure 1

Lower yourself onto your forearms and straighten your knees so you move your base of support to your forearms and feet (figure 1). Hold this position until you feel you are losing the neutral spine position and/or the co-contraction maneuver.

Gradually build up to the point at which you can hold the position for 30-60 seconds.

Repeat ________ times.

05 Lunge/Squat Track

EXERCISE **5.1** Forward Lunges

Stand comfortably with your arms at your sides (figure 1). Maintain the neutral spine position and the co-contraction maneuver.

Slowly step forward with your right foot, approximately one stride length (figure 2).

Slowly lower yourself until your knee lightly touches the ground (figure 3).

Slowly raise yourself up again and return to the starting position. Be sure to maintain the neutral spine position and the co-contraction maneuver while you do this. Repeat with the left leg.

Repeat ________ times on each side.

Figure 1

Figure 2

Figure 3

EXERCISE **5.2** Backward Lunges

Stand comfortably with your arms at your sides (figure 1). Maintain the neutral spine position and the co-contraction maneuver.

Slowly step backward with your right foot, approximately one stride length (figure 2).

Slowly lower yourself until your knee lightly touches the ground (figure 3).

Slowly raise yourself up again and return to the starting position. Be sure to maintain the neutral spine position and the co-contraction maneuver while you do this. Repeat with the left leg.

Repeat ________ times on each side.

Figure 1

Figure 2

Figure 3